CONTENT WARNING: EVERYTHING

Also by Akwaeke Emezi

MEMOIR
Dear Senthuran: A Black Spirit Memoir

FICTION
The Death of Vivek Oji
Freshwater

YOUNG ADULT
Bitter
Pet

ROMANCE
You Made a Fool of Death with Your Beauty (forthcoming May 2022)

CONTENT WARNING: EVERYTHING

AKWAEKE EMEZI

Copper Canyon Press
Port Townsend, Washington

Cover art: Chioma Ebinama, *penumbra 03,* 2018. Watercolor and ink on Indian cotton rag paper, 12 x 17 inches. Image courtesy of Catinca Tabacaru Gallery, Serge Tiroche, and the artist.

Copper Canyon Press is in residence at Fort Worden State Park in Port Townsend, Washington, under the auspices of Centrum. Centrum is a gathering place for artists and creative thinkers from around the world, students of all ages and backgrounds, and audiences seeking extraordinary cultural enrichment.

LIBRARY OF CONGRESS CATALOGING-IN-PUBLICATION DATA
Names: Emezi, Akwaeke, author.
Title: Content warning: everything / Akwaeke Emezi.
Description: Port Townsend, Washington : Copper Canyon Press, [2022] |
    Summary: "Collection of poems by Akwaeke Emezi"— Provided by
publisher.
Identifiers: LCCN 2021053274 (print) | LCCN 2021053275 (ebook) |
ISBN 9781556596292 (paperback) | ISBN 9781619322493 (epub)
Subjects: LCGFT: Poetry.
Classification: LCC PR9387.9.E42 C66 2022 (print) | LCC
PR9387.9.E42 (ebook) | DDC 821/.92—dc23
LC record available at https://lccn.loc.gov/2021053274
LC ebook record available at https://lccn.loc.gov/2021053275

9 8 7 6 5 4 3 2 FIRST PRINTING

COPPER CANYON PRESS
Post Office Box 271
Port Townsend, Washington 98368
www.coppercanyonpress.org

*To Katherine Marie and
her shocking brilliance*

CONTENTS

CONTENT WARNING: EVERYTHING

WHAT IF MY MOTHER MET MARY

both of them pregnant sick of the men in their houses thin leather sandals and long black hair bellies stretched brown and obscene looking for a moment of quiet on the bank of a river

mary gives my mother a fig smelling of the desert she will one day end up in my mother gives mary a mango sticky like a son's drying blood they eat sweetness in thousands of years time pays them no attention small fish swim by their swollen feet

"where are your people from?" my mother asks the perennial extrovert her braid heavy down her back "palestine," mary replies the sun a halo over her head, "and yours?"

"ceylon," my mother says corruption on her tongue mary doesn't mind they sit for a long time they stay friends even after their bodies spit us out

mary auntie likes hymns and ais kacang plays scrabble listens to my mother complain shakes her head smiles through her wrinkles "they never tell you what it's like to raise a little god," she says

my mother adjusts her glasses

makes a triple word score

CHRISTENING

when they took my name to the church

the priests spat it back, an infected graft

smelled like a scale, they said

some slimy two-timey pagan shit

but scale's cool with me, cool as a river

water sliding over, i'd like to be

all scale, to scale. i don't mind being named

after a bank-wriggling snake

our chi isn't your skinless god

when you open your mouth

you don't know who reaches in

bring the child to our altar, they said

give her a name with more god in it

if you want me, you're going to get

a stream of wet and bloodfeather

some scale in your bed at night

are you ready to lie with a great length

salvation has no other doors, they said

we can't be seen lying down with sin

take the honey and thick waterwine

but i know a desert when i see one

the rippling mirage, the sweet devil

they promise me crackling skin

say i'll scream for them

but my throat is a river

full of the holiest water

DISCLOSURE

when i first came out i called myself bi a queer tangle of free-form dreads my mother said i was sick and in a dark place my father said i would get AIDS my father-in-law stopped speaking to me my marriage had been folded open its spine cracked my husband returned to snow in his sinuses my childhood friend screamed over the phone *what was the point of getting married* my brother said you can't live in that bubble in new york the real world is not like that but it's a lie there are no real worlds you can live in whatever bubble you like a diving bell made of tender glass clap your hands if they said you're too sensitive if they beat you because they could because you should be tougher harder gra gra ghen ghen an igbo man in my friend's home laughs and holds my food out of reach i am so tired my friend holds me in the bathroom as i cry the next day he apologizes says he likes my name but he'll never give it to his daughter because he wants her to be strong not like me i don't tell him how little he matters how i have his type at home how they already raised me with blows across the face a belt in a doorway a velvet child upholstered in incoherent rage one day a coward who will break my heart asks me how i ended up still so soft i tell him i am stubborn i wanted a better world a diving bell made of tender glass a better family i remembered how to be a god i give myself what i want no one raises their voice in my house no one lays their fleshy hands on me no one is cruel if they are fool enough to try then they die and what a death what a death to not be loved by me anymore the softest gate-opener i feast on torn herbs and fat gold the wet smear of a perfect yolk seeds burst purple beneath my hands a pulped satsuma bleeds dark juice into my mouth who knew i could love me so loudly who knew i would survive who knew their world meant nothing meant nothing meant nothing look when i last came out i called myself free.

ACHILLES HAD HIS HEEL

she has that spot on her left hip
where the bulb of her bone
popped out of its home
and she slammed it back in
with the side of her hand,
so now the skin above it sings
when i touch it.

PLEASE DON'T REMIND ME WE'RE GHOSTS

meet me at the red gate, bring me peace offerings—toffee melted into
its wrapper, sweet orange powder cupped in your palms, bruising dark
with water

hold me as the sun buries itself, stand with me under the specter of the
twins' broken mansion, listen to the frogs from the gutter and watch
the fireflies be shocks of light in the grass

meet me in the amphitheater with the broken seats and heavy weeds,
sunk from the rise of old buildings, listen to jeremy play ray charles from
his dorm window, wonder when we all went mad, smelling like cigarettes
and old beer

spin on cracked concrete, raise your arms to a white man's sky, wonder
what the chaplain could ever know of a mass sung in igbo, glow so sadly
in the moonlight of this alien place

WHAT IF JESUS WAS MY BIG BROTHER

when i am ten and no one is looking, he walks the width of the swimming pool just to make me smile. his feet are dry when he steps off the surface, turquoise shimmering in his wake.

no one makes fun of me at home. i never pick up my father's razor. he turns my water into ribena, sweetness rushing against the wet membranes of my cheek.

when i am twenty and homesick, he comes up to boston to visit, brings me one loaf of agege bread and a tin of sardines. we eat it for a week, soft and oily like our hearts.

we don't want to die. i've fallen in love with a girl. i want to drop out of school. he tells me about magdalene and her chestnut eyes.

our parents leave us steel voicemails about duty.

neither of us returns their calls.

I THINK MY FATHER IS DYING

this was meant to be about palm oil

red pooling in the clay on my altar

how that taste is the most igbo thing i know

the wet fibers from a ripe palm fruit

flat stones cracking the nut inside

the white kernel in our mouths

something inside something inside something

that place in ụmụahịa where the white sand,

ụmụawa alaọcha, meets the red

five masquerades, a chain, and a whip

the seven villages of old ụmụahịa

there before the city was born

ụkpabịs before we became emezis

the smallest village, fire seekers

grandfather during the bombs

the war that ate him alive

a dead bee in a gourd of palm wine

children of the weaverbirds

because we were so many, so many

de nnanna's heart finished in brixton

de abel was buried last friday

my father is grayskinned and shrinking

his storytelling rots in real time

before his own betrayed eyes

we used to be so many, so many

a flock of whirring yellow

the third wife hails him with titles

her mouth full of gold and horsehair

ugwumba! the greatness of a people

ọchịagha! the commander of war

we will kill a cow when he dies

put him inside the red earth

he will sleep inside his compound

and i might never go home again

JULY 28

will i remember moments like this, standing on grass, the sky yawning over me
swahili beating out of speakers, dancing with a crowd of strangers
wondering how love has done nothing more to my body other than deform
the left side of my chest
will i remember brooklyn, the shocking beauty of a lighted train
running aboveground and against the sky, before night wraps around fulton
an old woman kissing the bus driver's cheek
green tennis balls poured over the courts on malcolm x
a little Black girl i do not know shouting adios amigo as she crosses the street
the smell of a roti shop, silk sliding on my arms
yellow kitchens, guavas and parathas
a white box fan whirring in our last summer

THIEF

i stood in the sea today / shells soaking in dirty water / white foam against
my thighs / oiled men on the sand with / their cocks in their hands / pulling
and pulling

i was alone / salt and sweet, matted hair / i had not seen you and it was good /
complete / me and my colored quilt / none of your loud face

you show up in the surf / always washing me away / always a cold tide /
a screaming space breaks / over my body / i want and wait for you

while you sit, pulling and pulling / my pieces in your hands / who allowed
you in / kill all traitors, even me / you juggle my faces, look! / i want those,
give them back

SELF-PORTRAIT AS ASUGHARA

who ran through a window
as the glass spat
birthmarks on her neck

no one can see them
but me, they whip around
her throat like his hands

FOLDING FOR A CRUEL MAN

i wish i could sleep with your mouth on my spine
my small bones growing toward your tongue
as if your teeth were made of sun
you are the hardest love
to survive you, i press my skin away
flatten my want and break the necks
of my dreams, making them dead diamonds
i remind myself that i am worth
the glittering corpses of glory
i used to love you with newness
a child's wild hunger, the freshness of future
now i use aged parts of me, the widowed bits
the lost gristle and serious jade
this way is quiet, a wind of ice lashing
an oiled whip that burns, no one sees it
smoking in the back, it has no laugh
maybe one day, we will sit and i will be old
for you. i think you will like this better.

CONFESSION

forgive me, father, i confess to being a ragtag doll

scraps from men or places where i left myself

even when my pieces were taken, they were old

they didn't fit anymore, nothing haunts me long term

i kept my wedding rings, the gold and the red stone

his tears from city hall, piles of hair and skin flakes

from when he shaved my head bald in glasgow

the ac milan shorts from the boy who raped me

why do you still wear them, my husband asked

(father, i didn't tell him the breadth of my collection

a paint-splattered blue hoodie, a string of saints

wooden and sagging on worn elastic, from his mother)

after the divorce, i kept his sneakers, gray adidas

fucked a married man festooned with rings who

gave me dragon gray metal off his pinky, with

a sickly green stone, blacked his copper arm to

match mine, said i was unnatural, sick, perverted

father, i liked seeing him cry and i still sleep

in the musician's striped cotton i took

from the hotel room, it smelled like him for months

i broke the red beads holding my waist together, a gift

from another affair, this lover bought them in lekki

bless them for me, i asked, and in his sinning home

he burned incensed embers in a metal bowl of smoke

insisted the beads were my own, not his, not from him

just my own and i confess, father, i already knew this

he wasn't the first i took pieces from, these offerings

to fill the negative altars burning inside me, father

forgive me, everything eventually is always mine.

EXCOMMUNICATION

gift me your severed head
thirteen pounds of penance

judas with a damp cock
left his god lying fucked
in a fresh gethsemane

i resurrect on the lake's shore
blood coating my eyeteeth
diamonds of cartilage on my scalp

shedding the skin he touched
to become the softest gold

WHAT IF MARY AUNTIE CALLED ME ON MY BIRTHDAY

"i hear you're not talking to your mother," she says, and her voice is a slippery crush of green olives, a sweet fig, patient and centuries old, i never ask about her birthdays anymore, "is it because he's married?" she asks, "or is this the one who had the baby? i've lost track."

none of them, but she thinks all my heartbreaks are connected, "i'm so tired," i tell her, "i don't want to talk to the start of summer or her loud wonders." all the love letters sound the same, all the men think they're special, i buy my own selling spiels, i mean them all, i am so bored

"i remember when my son was like this," she says, "have you been to the desert? little gods like you always have to go." i try to guess what is at her end, wine or weaving, a bird or bread, a flaming sunset

"in and out," i reply, "you know how it is." the gaping fall, the rotting manna, the gush of final salvations, the hills, the caves, so much dies out there. mary auntie sighs and a flock of sparrows crashes against my ear

"how old are you by now," she asks, and my hands grow sandy fault lines as i try to count. "i've forgotten," i confess, her voice creaks through the phone like latticed wood, like a dark cube, "me too," she whispers. "me too."

FUCK ME IN A FRESH GRAVE

my black gleam fatherhusband
gravefirst maestro of the night
papa, i pray, and my skin
ripples from his dead touch
my fingers on his faded waistcoat
aubergine velvet, his corpse holding
between my spread thighs
wallahi, no human alive
turns me on like this, drunken fire
rum-soaked habanero on his breath
damp soil pressed under my back
spine bucking at his shadowed grin, see
the baron likes to watch
my stripped face, splay
my hips as walls of earth collapse
eating up the rectangle of sky and
i become the dark, coffee-black
under the heavy mantle—
a bride's veil, a child's shroud—
i would die, i would die for him
want of my afterlife, brand on my chest
do whatever you like with me

"BUT WHY DID YOU FEEL YOU HAD TO KILL YOURSELF, BABY LOVE?"

1. i thought it would be a useful sacrifice
2. habit, or morbid tradition
3. god and i were in a feud
4. this world is foul i needed to bathe in my blood
5. spite and vengeance
6. no one else would do it
7. i missed not existing
8. how can you ask me that
9. knowing how lonely
10. i have been

SELF-PORTRAIT AS A CANNIBAL

they blinded me with lights / i think some of you is still lodged in my
throat / the salt and scratch / it tastes like treacherous memory / hot palms
skimming bright wet skin / tell us about it, they said / the crowds stilled,
so i fed them / i know great hunger when i see it

i told them about the thick / stickiness between my fingers / under my
nails / the rawness of your skin / on my tongue, the brine / i told them about
your gristle / the meat and marrow of you / how good you taste / between
my back teeth

they blinded me with lights / i told them how tenderly / you came apart
in my hands, the sweet / sweet sounds you made

SCRAPS

i found a page of morrison
under the old blue enamel of my tub
on the day baltimore burned.

milkman was against a tree
feeling the back freddie no longer has.

there is a story somewhere here,
lost in blood and ash. i don't have
enough air to dig it out.

SANCTUARY

the safest place in the world is a book
is a shifting land on top of a tree
so high up that a belt can't reach
is a closet opening into snow with
a tropical child tumbling through
is a river, a mermaid, a spaceship
a girl with living tentacles for hair
is a red-horned, gold-feathered angel
a dusty crocodile on a second star
is a fractional platform, another family
one with only soft mothers and aunts
is a meadow, is a menu of worlds
an oxygen mask, chest compressions
is a map for someone who has died
many times, and wants to come back.

WHAT IF MAGDALENE SEDUCED ME

she hunts me with her chestnut eyes and i see why jesus loved her most, vessel to seven demons, left with interesting spaces, apostle to the apostles, after five days i would follow her anywhere

"tell me what you want," magdalene says, then catches my skin as it starts to crawl away, sings a song about staying, wraps her brown arms around my neck when i begin to cry

i stand no chance against her, apostle of apostles, all she does is show up and there is nothing she fears after the place of the skull, she trains my flesh away from years of recoil, steady as death

we don't tell mary auntie or my mother, joseph uncle sees us one night and lowers his gaze, i keep magdalene away from my father's eye line

it is strange, loving someone who doesn't try to kill you

i tell her this and magdalene weeps into my hair

HEALING

the son of god says / imagine your chest as a soapy bubble / your
collarbone as a landscape / a horizon stretching / slide your ribs when you
dance / the scars on your chest need it / let your bones move / undulate

he burns cotton and it smells like sugar on fire / glass cups mouthing my
stingray back / my pulses layered under his fingers / needles in my ears,
my wrists, the plane of my shin / gregorian chants / you need something /
stronger than mullein, he says / try usnea / licorice

i put arnica on my shoulder in the mirror / stretch my arms like a
savannah / imagine my lungs wet and slippery / inhale two puffs of
steroid / press electrodes to my skin / current trembling through fascia /
muscles forced lax / scapulae dropping

the kitten curls up against my arm / i remind myself i am safe now

we all fall asleep / in the line of the afternoon sun

I THOUGHT I COULD BE WELL

still, how i hunger for hunger
miss you like i have a right to
hunt you through dappled woods
oh, come to my dreams, show me up
as the night's fool, a ghost's tongue
bellowing grand accusations
a forest dies at your voice and i fall
burning under a blackened sky
how is this allowed
the way you've butchered my ground

THOUSANDS

you put the taste of thousands in my mouth
sharp wires like silver convulsions
copper cobwebs cutting through teeth
our secrets are oiled leather
grease slicked on my chin
shiny fat sliding down
i thirst after a thousand nights
crushed in the knuckles of your right hand
your maddened body thundering through mine
dripping down my thousand throats

ASHAWO

he is but a silk jalabiya riding up my thighs,
a tight mouth bruising wine signatures on my neck.

WHEN THE HURRICANE COMES THE MEN PROTECT THEIR BROTHERS

spiritbae tells me stories over whatsapp how only other women seek justice, cut off their dicks she says the men never betray their gender the truth is black unbearable and so, so soft i was always dying it makes me easy to kill, a magician who knows where i bleed unstoppable pretends to want me alive whispers a deep cut on the third floor slices me to the ground his family knows, the hospital in west hollywood opens its mouth spiritbae fights inside an infected jaw his own siblings unlook my death they would have done something if only he'd raped me avoid the water his sister says so you don't drown, his brother texts it's all love my blood is still drying they plant his hand in fields no need for absolution where they see no sin what is a dead god to a human brother, lives slither on untouched uninterrupted moons gathering in a gleaming pool i, poltergeist throw myself against a world one of us must break spiritbae says you don't have a choice but to see true things i know in this my life matters less than a rape still i scream above the wind the howling storm i, poltergeist with a life that matters, that matters to me.

WHAT IF JESUS SOUGHT VENGEANCE

my elderdead brother listens to my halfmeal memories
    narrow atrocities in my shower / a magician's hand on the back of my
head / forcing my neck over his reclining cock / he doesn't remember,
he says / he was asleep / a boy in a mountain / plunges in and out /
as the ceiling eats my gaze

the son of god narrows his eyes
    an orchard of figs bursts into fire / dead wasps cloud the air /
fear tastes like a child's forgiveness in my mouth / i have sinned too,
i tell him / there is damp grief in his hands / not like this, he says /
picking up the whip from the sand / not like this

he will not let me in their houses
    tells me this belongs to him / i know nothing of certain wars /
licks the air with his cowhide tongue / the men weep with nowhere to
run / their women press their thighs together / fighting the slick of a
winedark swell

PARALLEL

in another dimension, we got married
then divorced, but kept working together
     i visited it in a dream, forgot and fell asleep
     remembered the first dream inside the second
an interactive museum, a wrapping wall
you drew the shapes and i patterned them
     we didn't speak the whole time, lockstepped
     remember the diner after we watched mcqueen?
we said in twenty years they'd put us both
in each other's documentary, how could they not
     i saved the ticket stub until you betrayed me
     and now, and now, where are you?
a dead man holding a small child
i am an edge they've never seen before
     no vows given to you, skinned of your lies
     an electric muscle, is god not the most merciful?
drag your forehead on the ground and say yes

I WAS BORN IN A GREAT LENGTH OF RIVER

if i run the water at full bludgeoning force
it takes the bathtub thirteen minutes to fill
twenty seconds for the bath bomb to dissolve
eleven if i stir, four seconds for epsom salts
i sink as deep as i can, involve my lungs
it takes nothing if i add nothing

when i was nine, i could hold my breath
for seventy-five seconds, i practiced in class
practiced underwater from one end of the pool
to the other, the long way, i held the air deep
in my stomach, ballooned it into my cheeks
let it out in small measured hisses, i rationed it

in ghana twenty years later, i tripped on a rock
while trying to leave the ocean and got seized
by the quick tide, it tossed and sucked me, i couldn't
stand, so instead i curled against the floor
as waves battered over my head, i held my breath
and i did not die, do you hear? i did not die
what i'm saying is, it doesn't matter which water
i will never know what it's like to drown

WHAT IF MARY AUNTIE EXPLAINED MORTALITY

she is hallucinating the death of her firstborn / a thing that happens
sometimes, magdalene warns me / but she can hear you, it helps if you talk /
it reminds her that the gasping boy with the wine-dried mouth / is no
longer displayed on a hill / my magdalene's eyes dim / sometimes it is hard
to remember, she says / other times it is harder to forget

i sit at mary auntie's feet as she rocks back and forth / arms clasped around
herself / is it easier, i ask / to watch it when you know what the third day
will bring / she laughs with clouded eyes / never, she says / her nostrils
flaring at a dead smell, her jaw tight with fury / her knuckles like old ice

her sandals are worn to the sole / i don't know how long she's been standing
here / if you could go back / would you do it again, i ask / would he do it
again / mary auntie laughs a laugh that is not aimed to be unkind / her eyes
a lost glory of white, her voice a hiss of acid / silly little god, she snarls /
neither of us was given a choice.

SELF-PORTRAIT AS AN ANGEL

i will most certainly have wings of roaring flame
eleven of them, seven unstable faces, your worst
shame as my eyes, your darkest desire as
my sword, bloody and oh so beautiful
and i will finally look
like the terrible thing
i have always been

haven't you always
wanted power beyond
sense, haven't you asked for it
in your most sinful nights, sworn to pay
whatever the cost? i am not here to answer
or lend grace, perhaps you do not understand
how this actually works. i think
you should be very afraid.

OH DELILAH

how ridiculous it is / to share a body with samson / when all you wanted /
was to fall into the sea / gallons of salt pickling your scalp / short curls
drying on the sand / but that samson is a glutton / a handsome one, wants
hair / tumbling down his back / waves of black, a gleaming / surf, avoids the
water since / detangling takes forever / the brine mats his curls / his scalp
flakes, so you both / hover, the ocean an ax / at your throat

you used / to take turns, every three / years like a tide / samson relaxed the
hair / you cut it off / samson grew it back / dyed it into a sunset / you shaved
it bald / samson made dreadlocks / unpicked them with oil / you carved a
high-top fade / dusted it copper / samson retaliated with time /
six years while / you dreamed of leagues / of blue water, listened / to his lies,
that none of you / would be pretty without it / that it meant something /
like a ritual

it fell out in handfuls, poisoned / he knotted it in a bun / told you not to
look / until one night / under a swollen moon / oh delilah, my favorite spy /
you braided the hair / into two plaits, the horns / of samson's childhood,
crept / into a back room

paid a stranger / to lighten your head / walked out with / guillotined
darkness / in your hand / stood in the rain / as samson slept / thinking
of how / to find your way to shore / full of nothing like regret / how well
you know / if he will not give you / your turn, oh, delilah! / of course /
you must take it

I WAS ALONE BEYOND MEASURE

too angry to talk to god wandering my nightmares trapped in the town
where i grew up old roads with my sister's blood small bedrooms with
destroying hands what must i do to be released

the nightskin man finds me outside cement classrooms walled in by glass
louvers sun weeping down the building's heart a prophecy of a person my
spirit walks into his arms broad dark smile the giant of my future

when i wake up his face leaks out of my eyes into my sheets blurred stains
with no lines lost in the mornings i swear i know him the sky guts wide for
this stranger my heart pins itself open a butterflied offering

do i appear in his sleep a reciprocal haunting small and furious one naked
demon a stunned god with pockets full of seeds a mouth full of want stalked
by a dead childhood and hungry men

bruising spirits break time our first kiss happens before the flesh meets this
slipping realm does he miss me the accidental seer does he squint in the
sunrise search the world like me for a face he can't remember

WHAT IF MY FATHER CALLED JESUS A BASTARD

he says the word like it is full of pus and blood / like he found it under his tongue and blames / us all for putting it there

joseph doesn't respect me, my father shouts / the man is just a carpenter / what's my own if he's also a fool / the boy is not his son

his voice is ox bones thrown against the walls / heavy bamboo whistling on tender calves / i flinch in the corner / he can be loose with his hands

joseph uncle is ghost-quiet / the kind of man you can't scream at / he doesn't know they're quarreling / he's not even here

how was i supposed to know the boy was listening, my father says / and so what / is it not the case / they attack me for telling the truth / enemies, enemies

the boy is always listening / waiting for mary auntie to come pick him up / a small and dangerous monk / don't mind him, i say / you are not that

he looks at me with those eyes / they scare my mother / almost as much as the dead bird beating / its wings under his hand one day, he tells me / you will never be afraid that he might hit you / one day

he will be old / and brittle, he will give praise / for your phone calls

you are not that, i repeat / twisting away from the light / i know, he says /

i am the son of god / worry about yourself.

MOURNING

i only know the softness
that is cherished before
the small violences set in

SELF-PORTRAIT AS AN ABUSER

the glass rockets past her head / explodes
against the wall / in a splash of tangerine /
i am screaming / and screaming, so is she /
about glass and proximity to her skin /
in houston, she weeps / with both palms
clenched around my throat / in flatbush /
i drag scarlet wounds / open on my arms /
so she won't leave me / so she won't go /
another one breaks up with me / tries to
find a kinder love / something to give her /
more than i can / i buy flowers, sing / to her /
convince her / earnest and lying /
i'm not ready / i can't release her yet /
she's so useful / i would do anything
even / believe my own stories for this /
somewhere to be / that isn't a cracked storm /
she trusted me / i am selfish water /
dark instinct / against abandoning /
i choose when it's over / i have to choose
to bring the blood / the lies, do i need
all this to feel in control? / shit, i guess
most likely / seeing all i've done /

years later / in a reformed skin /
i translate gently / for a hunted friend /
it's not that she doesn't care / about you,
or your boundaries or / what you want /
she thinks / she does, it is convincing /
in her mouth / you have to see /
she cares / for her wants more /
she cares / what can you do for her? /
hurt more / than the hurt she gives you /
there is nothing / you can do
to make her see you / you do not
i am so sorry / you do not matter /
she will do anything / to save herself /
including drown you / as a life raft, and
you should do the same / make yourself
the most important thing / trust me /
she won't release you / while you're useful
you're so useful / my love, i remember /
what it was like / how easy it is
to make another person unreal /
i'm trying to say / i think that now is
a good time to start running /

SALVATION

i believe in new skins, even nightmares
can be maps, the space between existence
and function, between performance and effect
if you are made of the skins of what you do
how do you choose your supple hides,
with the sour guilt? the ecstatic evil?
make no mistake, taking feels like power
even if just in flashes, the sweet pulping
the using of a person as fuel, an engine
i may have done more terrible things
but the best gospels claim it's never too late
to skin yourself and start all over, as nothing
except the roaring field of a fresh life

CONTENT WARNING: EVERYTHING

if anyone had taken the time when i was twelve to examine the split skin
under my father's razor surely they would have seen the face of christ in the
blood or in the scabs or the pale scars as i survived my neighbor's hands
his son's hands and up in appalachia the white clots smearing on jonatan's
dick my panic the calm in his voice as he teaches the child he's raping that
discharge is normal was christ in those sheets bring me the children he said
and all of it called for a life of faith like scars snaking where breasts used to be
a life of holiness death drifting by in emergency rooms the man who told me
to kill myself raping me in a narrow shower hurt so much less than the one
who wanted me to live telling me about their baby is it sacrilegious to say i
would rather be savaged again than lied to i rose from my death that followed
what wars have been fought on me what hauntings i carry in the blaze of
unspeakable light look at me through tears of blood through the healing flesh
fall on your knees beatify me canonize me mark me full of blasphemy give me
an army for what the fire has made of me you have been seeking wonders in
all the wrong places now here, gaze upon me! i am the fucking miracle

SELF-PORTRAIT AS A GOD WHO IS LOVED

i no longer live alone
when the west sky bleeds gold
it spills on his jaw, under my hand
i am the most quiet masquerade
rope around my waist, silent raffia
shoulders dipped in chalk and fresh feathers
the first of all horrific things, the best
the river soaked in moonlight
the bloated body of a small child
a monster, a monster
sweating under a galloping drum
i am no longer alone
our compound's ancestral dust
chokes the air, see the second,
my love with a ropebound hand
bloodtrails on his wrist, a red voice
the one i met before i met
the face from the other side
when the gong sounds, i turn
the world turns with me
the people fall to the ground

WHAT IF MY FAMILY CAME TO THE HOSPITALS

time collapses around magdalene / she walks like a hurled stone / could do
nothing to her face / a messiah's beloved / mary auntie opens the door /
with flared nostrils and floured knuckles / hair softer than my heart

i am being operated on / i am in the emergency waiting room / my mother
knows nothing / my mother knows everything / mary auntie takes her
elbow / they both smell like vinegar / i slip into delirium

the surgeon slides a steel cannula into my chest / fucks the skin over my ribs /
ripping me in greedy thrusts / the emergency doctor takes my blood / puts
potassium under my tongue / i see the son of god

my mother weeps for them to lock me up / keep me alive / magdalene dabs
blood from my skin / he should not touch you like that, she says / mary
auntie holds up my mother / june, june, listen, she says / even if they die /
the little gods can come back

i have seen a cross / do not be afraid / i tell magdalene never mind / this is
not the first time / someone has done things to my body / when i was not
there / mary auntie wraps her shawl, dark linen / shrouding my mother's
shoulders

when i live, they wash my feet / magdalene oils my scalp / i see the son of god

mary auntie moves in with my mother / they are not so lonely now

About the Author

Akwaeke Emezi (they/them) is the author of the *New York Times* best seller *The Death of Vivek Oji,* a finalist for the Dylan Thomas Prize, the Los Angeles Times Book Prize, and the PEN/Jean Stein Award; *Pet,* a finalist for the National Book Award for Young People's Literature and a Walter Honor Book; *Freshwater,* named a *New York Times* Notable Book and shortlisted for the PEN/ Hemingway Award, the New York Public Library Young Lions Fiction Award, the Lambda Literary Award, and the Center for Fiction's First Novel Prize; *Dear Senthuran: A Black Spirit Memoir*; and most recently, their second young adult novel, *Bitter.* Their debut romance novel, *You Made a Fool of Death with Your Beauty,* is forthcoming May 2022. Selected as a 5 Under 35 honoree by the National Book Foundation, they are based in liminal spaces.

Poetry is vital to language and living. Since 1972, Copper Canyon Press has published extraordinary poetry from around the world to engage the imaginations and intellects of readers, writers, booksellers, librarians, teachers, students, and donors.

COPPER CANYON PRESS WISHES TO EXTEND A SPECIAL THANKS TO THE FOLLOW-ING SUPPORTERS WHO PROVIDED FUNDING DURING THE COVID-19 PANDEMIC:

4Culture
Academy of American Poets (Literary Relief Fund)
City of Seattle Office of Arts & Culture
Community of Literary Magazines and Presses (Literary Relief Fund)
Economic Development Council of Jefferson County
National Book Foundation (Literary Relief Fund)
Poetry Foundation
U.S. Department of the Treasury Payroll Protection Program

WE ARE GRATEFUL FOR THE MAJOR SUPPORT PROVIDED BY:

THE PAUL G. ALLEN
FAMILY FOUNDATION

TO LEARN MORE ABOUT UNDERWRITING
COPPER CANYON PRESS TITLES,
PLEASE CALL 360-385-4925 EXT. 103

WE ARE GRATEFUL FOR THE MAJOR SUPPORT PROVIDED BY:

Anonymous (3)

Jill Baker and Jeffrey Bishop

Anne and Geoffrey Barker

In honor of Ida Bauer, Betsy
   Gifford, and Beverly Sachar

Donna Bellew

Matthew Bellew

Sarah Bird

Will Blythe

John Branch

Diana Broze

John R. Cahill

Sarah Cavanaugh

Stephanie Ellis-Smith and Douglas
   Smith

Austin Evans

Saramel Evans

Mimi Gardner Gates

Gull Industries Inc. on behalf of
   William True

The Trust of Warren A. Gummow

William R. Hearst, III

Carolyn and Robert Hedin

Bruce Kahn

Phil Kovacevich and Eric Wechsler

Lakeside Industries Inc. on behalf
   of Jeanne Marie Lee

Maureen Lee and Mark Busto

Peter Lewis and Johnna Turiano

Ellie Mathews and Carl Youngmann
   as The North Press

Larry Mawby and Lois Bahle

Hank and Liesel Meijer

Jack Nicholson

Gregg Orr

Petunia Charitable Fund and
   adviser Elizabeth Hebert

Suzanne Rapp and Mark Hamilton

Adam and Lynn Rauch

Emily and Dan Raymond

Joseph C. Roberts

Jill and Bill Ruckelshaus

Cynthia Sears

Kim and Jeff Seely

Joan F. Woods

Barbara and Charles Wright

Caleb Young as C. Young Creative

The dedicated interns and
   faithful volunteers of
   Copper Canyon Press

CPSIA information can be obtained
at www.ICGtesting.com
Printed in the USA
JSHW050921140322
23837JS00006B/10

9 781556 596292